Coal Man's Son

poems by

T. Crunk

Finishing Line Press
Georgetown, Kentucky

Coal Man's Son

Copyright © 2023 by Tony Crunk
ISBN 979-8-88838-105-2 First Edition
All rights reserved under International and Pan-American Copyright Conventions. No part of this book may be reproduced in any manner whatsoever without written permission from the publisher, except in the case of brief quotations embodied in critical articles and reviews.

Publisher: Leah Huete de Maines
Editor: Christen Kincaid
Cover Art: Public Domain
Cover Design: Russell Helms

Order online: www.finishinglinepress.com
also available on amazon.com

Author inquiries and mail orders:
Finishing Line Press
PO Box 1626
Georgetown, Kentucky 40324
USA

For Luca, always
For Peter, guide, fellow traveler

I lie awake;
I am like a lonely bird on the housetop.

—Psalm 102:7

one eyed bone
sees all you do

blind crow
tells it

Old Scratchfiddle
      plays the tune
Old Poorcoat
      dances—

I seen the man
        made of fire
in the driftmouth

        seen this
tree of lightning
        come walking
up out of the earth

        hellwind
cool and quiet
        as spilled water
soothing out
        behind him

seen him
        sidle down
the tracks apiece
        blind crow
on his shoulder
        one eyed bone
his staff
        tapping out his steps
along the crossties
        blind crow
singing
        old
blind crow song—

                fire burn
                ash fly

                spit a spark
                in your eye

seen them disappear
        around a bend
yon the turpentine woods
        ain't nothing
but thornbrush
        and jacktangle
all down
        in there anyway

sun goes down
       man made of fire
be up and about

       come down the road
looking in
       the windows
blind crow
       singing lullabies
singing
       for the children—

              O at night
              the sun slides
              under the hills

              to stoke
              the devil's
              furnaces

              that burn
              the belly
              of the earth

              to make
              the coal
              the miners dig

I seen
       old Strawboss Moon
up there though
       keeping his cool eye
out on everything

man made of fire
  say—

    blind crow
    bird of my

    grandfather's bones
    tell me

    what does
    the hellwind say

    soothing out
    the driftmouth

    cool and quiet
    as spilled water

    what does
    the hellwind say?

blind crow
  say—

    hellwind
    whispers

    O my
    children

    down in the bottom
    of the earth

           is a city
           a city made

           of blue bones
           and rock candy

           down in the flintrock
           down in the coalbreak
           down in the earthfire

           this is where
           your fathers

           go down
           this is where

           they go down

man made of fire
          say—

           O my
           one eyed bone

           hole in the earth
           so deep

           could be grave
           for many a man

how one eyed
  bone came to be:

flame
  from the driftmouth

then
  look up

see overhead
  man made of fire
up there
  riding the back
of old blind crow
  just
circling
  and circling

then bone
  broke open

bone
  broke open

out poured
  ten thousand years
of sorrow
  and salt

ten thousand years

  and then
that bone
  could see

man made of fire
      he lifted up
one eyed bone
      eye on a stalk

one eyed bone
      say—

            so far
            so good

            but up
            too far

            be up
            to no good

man made of fire
    say—

        one eyed bone
        go down

        in the earth
        come back

        tell me
        what do you see

one eyed bone
    say—

        ok chief

goes down
    in the earth
stay a little while
    come back up

man made of fire
    say—

        one eyed bone
        say what you seen

        down
        in the earth

        down there
        so deep

one eyed bone
    say—

        O
        I seen aplenty

        down
        in the earth

        so deep
        I seen

        the devil's
        butcher shop

        sign
        in the window

        say—

                Metes and Boans
                      Fresh
                Metes and Boans

bones
>> in the boneyard

bones all glowing
>> like radio tubes

calling to the flesh
>> waves in the air

blue waves
>> light waves

seeping down
>> washing

down
>> to the bones

bones
>> in the graveyard

all lit up
>> with tinsel lights

like Christmas
>> in town

but now
>> the question—

which station is it
>> that you
are going to
>> tune in to?

if old blind crow
        that old
iron bird
        come tapping around
your corner
        some evening
hat in his hand
        wanting to sell
you a ticket
        to a midnight
carnival
        you best just
turn that old
        bird away

if you hear
        thunder
in the night
        that be
old blind crow
        down in
the graveyard
        shooting dice
spitting for luck
        every time
he rolls them
        old devil bones

if you hear
        a lost hound
baying out
        all up Dry Branch
that might just be
        a lost hound

baying out
        all up Dry Branch
but it might too
        be old blind crow
off in the brushwood
        wailing out his grief
for all the lost worlds
        here and to come
that old one eyed bone
        told him he seen

old blind crow
        off in the brushwood
wailing out his grief
        for all
the lost worlds
        here and to come

singing out
        the oldest old
crow song
        they is—

                O bones
                bones

                go down
                in the earth

                line up
                the boxcar caskets

                mile after mile
                no end in sight

                bonetrain
                going down

                the manway
                down the hole

                at the bottom
                of the earth

                no end to it

                no caboose

I seen
        a bullethole
in the cross
        atop
Spring Hill Church

        seen old
one eyed bone
        peeking out of it

old blind crow
        old hurdy
gurdy bird
        down on
the streetcorner
        do a little step
tip his hat
        say—

                afternoon
                ladies and gents

then sing
        old crow song
sing
        the one about
Old Scratchfiddle
        fiddles a tune
Old Poorcoat
        dances

sing so sweet
        he try to
make you forget
        you seen him
night before
        down on
the creekbank
        picking his
way down
        behind the
ferryman's shack
        try to make
you forget
        you seen him

    kneel down
           in the bulrushes
there
       take a sip
of creekwater
        seen that
creekwater there
         turn to ashes

man made of fire
        stop me
in the road
        one time

say—

                anybody here
                want to dance

                this dance

                how about
                you

                boy?

bone
        in the holy ghost
bone
        in the flesh
bone
        in the mudmeat

rattling bone
        clattering
like dirt
        on a coffin lid

one eyed bone
        say—

                O what can hold
                the darkness out?

                bones
                and nothing but

                only
                the rim bones

                of nothing
                hold the dark out

                only the cage bones
                of night

man made of fire
    come walking
in the boneyard
    one eyed bone
calling—
    O my brothers
blind crow
    pecking out a tune
on a grin
    tooth skull

man made of fire
    knows the recipe
for blood

    calls for
a big iron kettle
    black as the hole
at the bottom
    of the earth

build a big fire
    underneath

man made of fire
    say—

        blood
        is love

        and a fistful
        of mud

        stir him around
        stir him around

O mudmeat baby

croon and sing
croon and sing

stick a bone in him
stand him up

O mudmeat baby
croon and sing

spit a spark
in his eye

so he can see
spit a spark

in his mouth
so he can speak

but don't spit
no spark

in his ear

ain't nothing
we're saying

he needs to hear

        O
little

        mudpuppet
bloodboy

        needs him
a name

        lookit
dancing

        think I'll
call him

        god jesus

bone broke open
        ten thousand years
poured out
        black fire
of sorrow
        and salt
I gathered up
        in my own
two
        white hands

man made of fire
        say—

                now you got him
                what to do with him?

I say—

        rock him
        like a baby

        rock him
        rock him

        rock him
        down easy

        away
        down easy

        rock him

        rock him

god jesus
        mudbaby
say—

                goodbye mother
                mother bed

                hello father
                father coffin

                short life
                a trouble

                in between

god jesus
        bloodboy
say—

                O
                travel light

                in this world

                rest well
                in the next

man made of fire
    go back in his hole
back down
    to the bottom of the earth

just turn and go

    blind crow
one eyed bone
    go with him

ring of fire
    around his feet
black pool of fire
    around and around
just circling
    and circling

down they go
    down and down

I looked
    down in that
hole of fire
    I seen
all hell devils
    dancing a circle
a circle of fire
    all smoke
and serpents
    a fire
around a fire
    fire in the atoms
circling
    and circling

atom holes
．．．．．in the air
adam holes
．．．．．．in the dark

bone broke open
        sputtering black fire

spewed out
        emptied—

at last
        clear music

bone flute
        cool and quiet

in a world
        now

burning

and what does
        the hellwind say
deacon
        soothing out
the driftmouth
        cool and quiet
as spilled water
        what
does the hellwind say?

hellwind
        say—

                The Tempter
                is the one eyed bone

hellwind
        say—

                That firetrain
                done raced home
                to the shot

bone broke open
all sorrow and salt

pouring out
black fire

a ring
a fire

go down
clean white

down to the bottom
wall of paper

and you

began to speak
ten thousand years

pool of fire
poured out

about my feet
I would enter

and down
into the fire

white as this
between me

drill two holes
in my coffin lid

if the devil
slips in one

I'll slip
out the other

www.ingramcontent.com/pod-product-compliance
Lightning Source LLC
Chambersburg PA
CBHW022122090426
42743CB00008B/971